100

THINGS TO DO IN
KANSAS
CITY
BEFORE YOU
DIE

100
THINGS TO DO IN
KANSAS
CITY
BEFORE YOU
DIE

● ●

TRACI ANGEL

REEDY PRESS

Reedy Press
PO Box 5131
St. Louis, MO 63139, USA
www.reedypress.com

Library of Congress Control Number: 2014957687

ISBN: 9781935806899

Design by Jill Halpin

Printed in the United States of America
14 15 16 17 18   5 4 3 2 1

Please note that websites, phone numbers, addresses, and company names are subject to change or cancellation. We did our best to relay the most accurate information available, but due to circumstances beyond our control, please do not hold us liable for misinformation. When exploring new destinations, please do your homework before you go.

CONTENTS

xiii • **Preface**

xvii • **Acknowledgments**

2 • **Food and Drink**

3 • Nosh at a Gas Station

4 • Eat with a Conscience at Anton's Taproom

5 • Nibble a Long John or Cake Donut

6 • Look for Ghosts at Belvoir Winery

8 • Elbow Your Way to Artisan Chocolate and Ice Cream

10 • Jump with Local Java

12 • Twirl Pasta Like in the Old Country

13 • Dive at the Diners

14 • Imbibe Local Beer

16 • Make Your Own Sausage

17 • Grab a Bier the German Way

18 • Need a Wee Bit of Something Irish?

19 • Trek for Tortillas

20 • Go Abroad for a Cup or Bite

21 • Dine at the Central Terminal

23 • Mooove Like You Mean It

24 • Celebrate Local Brew in the West Bottoms

25 • Slurp Frou-Frou Drinks with Style

26 • Barbecue—Of Course!

28 • Soul Food That's Good for the, Well, Soul

30 • **Music and Entertainment**

32 • Rock on the Porch

33 • Catch a Show and Meal

34 • See a Moonlight Production

35 • Hail, and Well Met!

36 • Listen to All That Jazz

39 • Be Part of the Crowd

40 • Get Your Craic On

42 • For Art's Sake

44 • Try an Alfresco Viewing

46 • Hold Your Breath!

47   **Sports and Recreation**

48   See the City by Bike

49   When in KC

50   Get Lost in Swope Park

52   Feed the Fish and Ducks at Longview

53   Hike in Quiet

54   Feed the Goats

55   Have a Wild Time

56   Get Away

57   Stroll an Urban Garden

58   Sink One In

59   Take Time for the Rodeo

60   Sled Down Like You Know What's Up

61   Indulge in Some Royal Treatment

62   Be a Fútbol Fan

63   Pick Your Own

64   Take Yourself Out to the Ballgame

65 • Observe Jayhawks in Their Natural Habitat

66 • Find Out About All the Hoopla

67 • Bleed Red

68 • Make a Splash and Defy Gravity

69 • **Natural Beauty**

70 • Cross the Prairie

72 • Find an Urban Oasis

73 • Head for the Farm

74 • Cheer on the Kangaroos

76 • Fly Above an African Savannah

79 • **Culture and History**

80 • Study the Public Murals

82 • Let Your Hair Down

83 • Hop a Ride on a Street Car

84 • Get to the Top

85 • Drive Through Whimsical Nutterville

86 • Remember

87 • Pay Your Respects to Charlie "Bird" Parker

88 • Study American Indian Influence

89 • Learn More About the African-American
Pioneers at Bruce Watkins

90 • Walk Where the Outlaws Did

91 • Peek at the Shady Past

92 • Explore in the Footsteps of Lewis and Clark

93 • Watch the Flames

95 • See Pigs Race

96 • Walk Back in Time

97 • Peek Inside an Artist's Studio

98 • Brush Up on Design

99 • Go Mod for Art

100 • Bump Your Nose on the Glass

• •

101 • Find Inner Peace

102 • Show Up for the Show

103 • Tour a Throwback Town

104 • Learn About the Mormon Settlement

105 • Scat Like You Mean It

106 • See Civil War–Era Architecture

107 • Roll with the Hogs

108 • Take a Big-League Tour

109 • Find Your Story

110 • Watch in a World-Class Way

111 • Hail to the Chief

112 • Uncover a Treasure

113 • It's Electric

114 • Look Up Something

115 • Roll in the Dough

116   **Shopping and Fashion**

117   Be Seen at the Scene

118   Get the Blues

119   Wear Your Heart on Your Shirt

120   Head for Fashion

121   Go Under

122   Grab Culture in the Suburbs

123   Hang with the Hipsters

124   Read Like a Child

125   Stride Through the Plaza

126   Eat Local and Fresh

128   Shop for Throwback Threads and Spots to Pop a Squat

129   **Suggested Itineraries**

133   **Activities by Season**

135   **Index**

PREFACE

Maybe I'm one of those crazy little women the song is talking about.

I lived in Kansas City as a single young person and returned as we started our family. I'm a Missouri girl, though, and the fact that I grew up elsewhere often works to my advantage as a writer because I venture beyond old haunts or personal history. I see newness through the lens of transplant eyes. And I ask a lot of questions.

Often when we got into the car of a morning my toddler son would ask, "Where are we going today, Mommy?" We called them "adventures." I found that the best way to learn about a place is to just go and talk to people. And then we'd go to other places based on recommendations. I realize much of the following list was filed in the back of my mind—a little light going on whenever we tried a different event in a different part of town—even before I signed the book contract.

Here's the thing about Kansas City: just when you think you have it pegged for a super-friendly fly over city, you discover how the city's niceness includes a seedy, gangster past in which speakeasies and gambling parlors were endemic during Prohibition. You can write off Kansas suburbanites as conservative churchgoers and then find them to be the fiercest soccer fans—far ahead of the rest of US fans.

• •

Another thing about Kansas Citians is that we do appreciate culture and there's a completely different Kansas City than the "cow town" wild-west version often portrayed. Since Kansas City was dubbed "Paris of the Plains" during its jazz heyday the city has kept that focus, most recently demonstrated in the building of the Kaufmann Center for the Performing Arts that beautifully underscores the city's skyline and brings world-class acts to town.

We love barbecue, our families, and eating barbecue with our families while enjoying a low cost of living. Oh, and you can't help but like us, because even though we are sensitive to challenging racial, rural-versus-urban, Missouri or Kansas, my-state-college-is-better-than-your-state-college, and historically questionable American Indians and slavery issues, we also like to poke fun at our Midwestern roots and our unlikely coolness.

Two notes about the book:

1. Some attractions lie beyond the city proper and into the suburbs and even to places nearly an hour away. Kansas City is like that. A major university (University of Kansas) is in nearby Lawrence, and other must-dos in the Heartland are of the agrarian variety, so you gotta get out of Dodge. (Metaphorically speaking, of course, because this book does not take you all the way to Dodge City, Kansas. That's just crazy talk.)

2. Be sure to make a phone call or check before you go, because restaurants and establishments change and evolve with little warning and ongoing events could change by the time you pick this up. Please do your homework, and we will try to update as much as possible when we can.

Kansas City, here you come.

ACKNOWLEDGMENTS

Thank you to Mark O'Hara, Jennifer Weaver, Clayton Bellamy, D.J. Wilson, Sarah Shipley, Robin Turley, Dennis Ridenour, Monica and David Kissick, Porter and Cheryl Arneill, Elaine Adams, Friday Morning Shepherd's Center Meals on Wheels volunteers, my smart and funny girlfriends of Again with the Book Club and all the Facebook and Twitter peeps who helped along the way. I also appreciate the other *100 Things to Do* writers paving the road, including Amanda E. Doyle in St. Louis, who started it all. And, of course, much love to my family for their support, and to my fellow local tourists, Zara, Jack, and Jason, who are always up for an adventure.

100

THINGS TO DO IN
KANSAS
CITY
BEFORE YOU
DIE

FOOD AND DRINK

NOSH
AT A GAS STATION

We know there is a joke in here somewhere about eating at a place known for getting gas. Barbecue king Joe's Kansas City (formerly Oklahoma Joe's) shares a door with a convenience store that can be seen from its tables. Joe's Kansas City serves up the Z-Man sandwich—brisket with an onion ring on top. Papu's, a Mediterranean café inside a Shell station, offers falafel and hummus among its other entrees. Its tables sit a few feet from the refrigerated bottled soda. Pizza 51 West on the University of Missouri-Kansas City campus still looks like a gas station, but is without pumps and other store items. Order the "Cowtown Lovers" all-meat pie, an appealing bang for your buck for all carnivores.

Joe's Kansas City (formerly Oklahoma Joe's): 3002 West 47th Avenue, Kansas City, KS 66103
913-722-3366
www.joeskc.com

Papu's: 604 West 75th Street, Kansas City, MO 64114
816-822-8759
Neighborhood: Waldo

Pizza 51 West: 5060 Oak Street, Kansas City, MO 64112
816-531-1151
www.pizza51.com
Neighborhood: UMKC campus

EAT WITH A CONSCIENCE
AT ANTON'S TAPROOM

Knowing where the food comes from is serious business here. They raise their own tilapia in the aquaponics system downstairs. The nutrients from the fish waste help feed herbs and lettuce growing on top of the tank. Owners take care in checking out meat providers to ensure quality. Wash down the meal with one of the beers from the restaurant.

Anton's Taproom: 1610 Main Street, Kansas City, MO 64108
816-888-8800
www.antonskc.com
Neighborhood: Crossroads

NIBBLE
A LONG JOHN OR CAKE DONUT

Go on a quest to find your favorite so you can add your perspective to the debate on the best donut shop. Aside from barbecue, Kansas Citians like to argue about the best place to stop for fried dough in the mornings. LaMar's, a city favorite, sells out its Valentine's Day red velvet donuts before the end of morning rush hour. Along Stateline Road is Fluffy Fresh, unassuming in a strip mall with "DONUTS" marked overhead. The area abounds with independent mom-and-pop shops with their spin on glazed, sugared, iced, and sprinkled. People swear by John's Space Age Donuts for the taste with differing opinions of snark and sincere service. We just like the idea of it.

LaMar's:
www.lamars.com

Fluffy Fresh Donuts: 10123 State Line Road, Kansas City, MO 64114
816-942-9822

John's Space Age Donuts: 8124 Floyd Street, Shawnee Mission, KS 66204
913-381-0980

LOOK FOR GHOSTS
AT BELVOIR WINERY

An old, odd district seems like, well, an odd place for a winery, but Dr. John L. Bean and his wife, Marsha transformed the historic property into a destination nearly two decades ago. They took what served as an administration building in the Liberty location and created a wine-processing facility—Belvoir Winery. Local artists hang displays, and the grounds are a popular location for events and weddings. One of the more popular events involves looking for paranormal activity through expert-guided tours.

Belvoir Winery: 1325 Odd Fellows Road, Liberty, MO 64068
816-200-1811
www.belvoirwinery.com

INSIDER TIP

*Murder mystery dinners—
hosted regularly—are sold
out well in advance, so book
them early. You can bring your
own ghost-hunting gear for the
paranormal tours.*

ELBOW YOUR WAY
TO ARTISAN CHOCOLATE AND ICE CREAM

Christopher Elbow, who grew up in nearby Liberty, makes chocolates that might be an elixir for a sweet tooth. He is the pastry chef for the American Restaurant, and his chocolates are a major draw here. You'll find his influence in other Kansas City favorites, too, like the chocolate ale he helped create with Boulevard Brewing that has people lining up in stores for its annual release. Another of Elbow's culinary endeavors is Glacé Artisan Ice Cream, which brings customers for after dinner treats in whimsical flavors of cucumber-lime sorbet, goat cheese and wildflower honey, and basil and French lavender.

Christopher Elbow Artisanal Chocolates: 1819 McGee,
Kansas City, MO 64108
816-842-1300
www.elbowchocolates.com

Boulevard Brewing: 2501 Southwest Boulevard, Kansas City, MO 64108
816-474-7095
www.boulevard.com/BoulevardBeers/chocolate-ale/

Glacé Artisan Ice Cream: 4960 Main Street, Kansas City, MO 64112
816-561-1117
www.glaceicecream.com

INSIDER TIP

Those looking for flavorful ice cream with a more traditional flair should go to Murray's in Westport. They continually update their flavors and put creative, local twists on the dessert, such as the Kansas City Cheesecake flavor. People who have moved far from the midtown area still make the trip back for dessert. Homemade cookies and fresh coffee complement the icy treats.

Murray's Homemade Ice Creams
4120 Pennsylvania Avenue
Kansas City, MO 64111
816-931-5546
Neighborhood: Westport

JUMP
WITH LOCAL JAVA

You can cross off a couple of these things to do in the same day if you are properly caffeinated. Lucky for you we know where to go. May we suggest:

Oddly Correct—Where they will deliver beans by bicycle if you wish. They take their coffee seriously and have a diehard following. They are in the cool part of town, but don't call them hipsters.

The Roasterie—This brand is a local favorite for cafeterias and restaurants, with a few cafés around town, including one in quaint Brookside that invites people to come in but not stay too long.

Parisi—Also found in downtown spots and has diehard fans. Parisi houses a café in the architectural wonder that is Union Station.

Coffee Girls—This modern shop looks out of place in the mismatched zoning of Waldo, but it has friendly baristas and a warm vibe despite its industrial interior. Insider Tip: Try the juices and smoothies— clever combinations that include carrot, kale, and beet.

City Market Coffee House—Get your buzz to carry you through your River Market farmer's market shopping. It's a cozy find amid the other standing market stores. A breakfast burrito—including veggie and vegan options—can give you more energy for your shopping.

Oddly Correct: 3940 Main Street, Kansas City, MO 64111
816-555-5555
www.oddlycorrect.com

Roasterie: 6223 Brookside Boulevard, Kansas City, MO 64113
816-333-9700
www.theroasterie.com

Parisi: 30 West Pershing Road, Union Station, Kansas City, MO 64108
913-569-2399
www.parisicoffee.com

Coffee Girls: 7440 Washington Street, Kansas City, MO 64114
816-221-2326
www.kccoffeegirls.com

City Market Coffee House: 305 Main Street, Kansas City, MO 64105
816-718-3005
www.citymarketcoffee.org

TWIRL PASTA
LIKE IN THE OLD COUNTRY

The owner, Michael Garōzzo, cut his Italian cuisine teeth on St. Louis's famous "Hill" Italian neighborhood, where he was born and raised. He made it to Kansas City and replicated his version of the family-style-we-remember-you. His chicken spiedini is the local favorite, and now he has multiple locations throughout Kansas City.

Garōzzo's Ristrorante: 526 Harrison Street, Kansas City, MO 64106

816-221-2455

www.garozzos.com

DIVE
AT THE DINERS

Sometimes you just want a greasy hamburger and an atmosphere with some character and perhaps a few characters. Town Topic near the Crossroads district has a loyal following of lunchtime diners, but it brings all kinds after hours when happy-hour goers need something to sop up the booze in their bellies. It gets its fair share of accolades for food items and its legacy.

Locals view Winstead's as their fast-food joint. The franchise, located in the Kansas City area, has been around for more than seventy years. The steak burgers come from a local meat company, and you use your spoon to drink the milkshake here. Food writers like Calvin Trillin, who grew up in Kansas City, and other media have named this the best hamburger around.

Town Topic: 2021 Broadway Street, Kansas City, MO 64108
816-842-2298
www.towntopic.com

Winstead's: 101 Emanuel Cleaver II Boulevard, Kansas City, MO 64112
816-753-2244
www.winsteadssteakburger.com

IMBIBE
LOCAL BEER

Boulevard established its name and bolstered a reputation when it became Kansas City's hometown beer in 1989. But twenty-four years later founder John McDonald sold it to Belgian company, Duvel, who insists they'll keep its focus in Kansas City. Other microbrews bring their own game. Establishments like 75th Street Brewery, Martin City Brewery, and McCoy's offer restaurant space to enjoy the local beverage. Also check beer lists for batches from Cinder Block Brewery and Rock and Run Brewery up north.

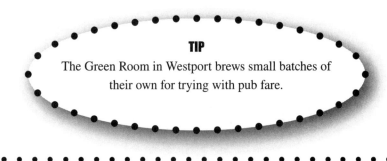

TIP
The Green Room in Westport brews small batches of their own for trying with pub fare.

Boulevard Brewery: 2501 Southwest Boulevard,
Kansas City, MO 64108
816-474-7095
www.boulevard.com

75th Street Brewery: 520 West 75th Street,
Kansas City, MO 64114
816-523-4677
www.75thstreet.com

Martin City Brewery: 500 East 135th Street,
Kansas City, MO 64145
816-268-2222
www.martincitybrewingcompany.com

McCoy's: 4057 Pennsylvania Avenue,
Kansas City, MO 64111
816-960-0866
www.mccoyspublichouse.com

Green Room Burgers & Beer: 4010 Pennsylvania Avenue,
Kansas City, MO 64111
816-216-7682
www.greenroomkc.com

Cinder Block Brewery: 110 East 18th Avenue,
North Kansas City, MO 64116
816-298-6555
www.cinderblockbrewery.com

Rock & Run Brewery and Pub: 110 East Kansas Street,
Liberty, MO 64068
816-415-2337
www.rockandrunbrewery.com

MAKE
YOUR OWN SAUSAGE

If you are local and all about eating close to home with ingredients that were raised and slaughtered close to home, you know about The Local Pig. This is an old-fashioned butcher shop with a modern twist—they make sure the meat you buy is humanely raised and also provide an opportunity for a self-aware approach to meat-eating.

The Local Pig: 2618 Guinotte Avenue, Kansas City, MO 64120
816-200-1639
www.thelocalpig.com
Neighborhood: East Bottoms

TIP
Take a butchering class to learn about breaking down animals to create your own meat products.

GRAB A BIER
THE GERMAN WAY

Those wanting their beer, or bier, with an international flair should head to Waldo, a south-central neighborhood. Within blocks are two bier-drinking hubs. Tall convenience-store refrigerators line one wall of The Bier Station, with bottles imported from afar that will entice most beer enthusiasts. Take some home or join others in soaking up the brews on tap paired with local Farm to Bakery pretzels, baked a few blocks away. A little farther south is KC Bier Company, which opened in 2014. The owner, German bier expert Steve Holle, brings his recipes to the biergarten and tasting room. Its insides reflect Deutschland's brew hall influence, and when you have a Pilsner in hand, the wooden patio furniture next to the neighborhood bike trail might as well be Bavaria. Both places are kid friendly, with The Station offering children's sized "Root Bier Station" T-shirts. The Bier Company's patio is complete with a wooden playhouse that blends with the motif. Probst!

The Bier Station: 120 East Gregory Boulevard, Kansas City, MO 64114
816-548-3870
www.bierstation.com

KC Bier Company: 310 West 79th Street, Kansas City, MO 64114
816-214-8691
www.kcbier.com

NEED A WEE BIT
OF SOMETHING IRISH?

So ya wanna bit of history, do ya, laddie? In the late eighteen hundreds the great ancestor of what is now Browne's traded traditional Irish embroidered lace and hams for pennies. Places like these, passed down through four generations just don't exist anymore. Try soaking up the brews paired with local baked goods. Try the Reuben.

Browne's Irish Market: 3300 Pennsylvania Avenue, Kansas City, MO 64111
816-561-0030
www.brownesmarket.com
Neighborhood: Midtown

TREK
FOR TORTILLAS

A cruise down Southwest Boulevard leaves no shortage for options of the Hispanic variety. Just when you think you should be turning around, keep going and you'll likely find a small shop or restaurant you missed before. At Margarita's Amigos it seems only fitting, perhaps necessary, to try the margarita. Do so—you won't regret it. Sabor Y Sol is another favorite, and others rave about the Mexican brunch at Poco's.

Margarita's Amigos: 2829 Southwest Boulevard, Kansas City, MO 64108
816-326-7421
www.margaritasamigos.com

Sabor Y Sol: 542 Southwest Boulevard, Kansas City, KS 66103
913-362-0817

Poco's: 3063 Southwest Boulevard, Kansas City, MO 64108
816-931-2526
www.pocosontheblvd.com

GO ABROAD
FOR A CUP OR BITE

OK, so you're in the middle of the United States. Paris is a twelve-hour plane ride away, but you want something a little European. Crestwood is a short stretch of shopping between Oak and Brookside, just south of the Plaza. Try Café Europa for brunch or something sweet to go with your coffee. Aixois Bistro creates the rich, French dishes that stay with you and make you consider shopping for art and poodles.

Café Europa: 323 East 55th Street, Kansas City, MO 64113
816-523-1212
www.cafeeuropakc.com

Aixois Bistro: 251 East 55th Street, Kansas City, MO 64113
816-333-3305
www.aixois.com

DINE
AT THE CENTRAL TERMINAL

Union Station is a destination in itself. The architectural great was built in 1914 and has 850,000 square feet of space. Walking into it can take one back to days when trains whistled through the city. Locals know Union Station for another reason—Pierpont's is considered one of the best fine-dining experiences with reasonable prices. The food is classic-style steak and seafood. This is also a favorite lunch spot for many who are looking for an upscale menu. Try it before checking out one of Union Station's traveling exhibits or perhaps before heading to nearby Crown Center or the Crossroads District.

Pierpont's: 30 West Pershing Road, Union Station, Kansas City, MO 64108
816-221-5111
www.pierponts.com

MOOOVE
LIKE YOU MEAN IT

A trip to most supermarkets in Kansas City can result in purchasing flavored milk in throwback glass bottles from Shatto Milk Company. The dairy farm and bottling operation is an hour north of Kansas City, and while it is big enough to cater to needs in a hundred-mile radius, it's also small enough to offer tours nearly every day. Take the tour! It's worth the trip to see the cows in their element, watch the milking and bottling process and then sample the latest flavor—banana, coffee, cotton candy, root beer—the company has to offer. If you start looking you'll find that Shatto milk is a key ingredient at local restaurants and cafés.

Shatto Milk: 9406 Missouri Highway 33, Osborn, MO 64474
816-930-3862
www.shattomilk.com

CELEBRATE LOCAL BREW
IN THE WEST BOTTOMS

Boulevardia in the Crossroads began in the summer of 2014 and is sure to become a popular festival among the local beer, Boulevard Brewing Company, and music crowds. The combination of tunes and brew brings a younger, hipper crowd to a venue that itself is worth a trip. Any venture to the West Bottoms beckons the spirits of the Irish and German laborers who lived together under the rule of mob boss Tom Pendergast in the late 1920s and early 1930s. The gravelly parking lots and the worn brick warehouses keep the secrets in as the mind wanders to the shadows of how the city lived under the mobster's rule.

Boulevardia:
www.boulevardia.com

SLURP
FROU-FROU DRINKS WITH STYLE

It's OK to sit back with something icy and pink of the alcoholic variety at Snow and Company. Its location in the arty Crossroads District gives it street cred, but the drinks speak for themselves. So go ahead and try the Pink Slipper, which is 360 Vodka infused with ginger, fresh grapefruit, and agave simple syrup, but is so delightfully sweet it might as well include babies' tears and first kisses. For something a bit more grown up, go for the Sunshine Boulevard. It hits a welcome sour note using local beer Boulevard Wheat, orange juice, and vodka.

Snow and Company: 1815 Wyandotte Street, Kansas City, MO 64108
Neighborhood: Crossroads

Gladstone 18 Building, 504 NE 70th Street, Gladstone, MO 64118
www.snowandcompany.com

BARBECUE—OF COURSE!

The spicy sauce and smoking goodness of meat often brings people together here in Middle America. It also can tear them apart. Where do you begin to tell people to go in a town where even suburban dads try their skills in barbecue tournaments? The mighty four, by local standards, are Arthur Bryant's, Gates, Joe's Kansas City (formerly Oklahoma Joe's), and Fiorella's Jack Stack Barbecue (an older location is in Martin City, not the Plaza). But look around, off the beaten path, and you'll find some roadhouse, suburban places, such as RJs Bob-Be-Que Shack in Mission, Kansas; Rosedale Barbeque; or Woodyard Bar-B-Que in Kansas City, Kansas. The locations are as original as their creative spellings of barbecue. Others, like Q39, try an artisan spin on the local cuisine. We are prepared for arguments, but after some research and polling we came up with these top entries for two categories.

TIP

Do not trust an experience at Arthur Bryant's at Kansas City International Airport or at any shopping area. Make the trip to the northeast city location on Brooklyn Avenue.

Best Burnt Ends

LC's Bar-B-Q: 5800 Blue Parkway, Kansas City, MO 64129
816-923-4484

Gates & Sons Bar-B-Q: 2001 West 103rd Terrace, Leawood, KS 66206
913-383-1752
www.gatesbbq.com

Arthur Bryant's: 1727 Brooklyn Avenue, Kansas City, MO 64127
816-231-1123
www.arthurbryantsbbq.com

Best Blue Collar Barbecue

Arthur Bryant's: 1727 Brooklyn Avenue, Kansas City, MO 64127
816-231-1123
www.arthurbryantsbbq.com

RJ's Bob-Be-Que Shack: 5835 Lamar Avenue, Mission, KS 66202
913-262-7300
www.rjsbbq.com

Rosedale Barbeque: 600 Southwest Boulevard, Kansas City, KS 66103
913-262-0343
www.rosedalebarbeque.com

Woodyard Bar-B-Que: 3001 Merriam Lane, Kansas City, KS 66106
913-362-8000
woodyardbbq.com

SOUL FOOD
THAT'S GOOD FOR THE, WELL, SOUL

When the women at a YMCA aquacise class suggest a pregnant woman must try Peachtree Buffett, you have to take their word for it. Peachtree describes itself as "soul food with elegance," but you won't find pretension here. Instead, it's home-cooked fried chicken and catfish and a rotating buffet menu. Everything about the place makes you think you are dining with your fun and sophisticated auntie. For more low-key soul food, many locals go to Niecie's, which has been voted one of the best breakfast spots in Missouri and is especially known for its chicken and waffles, which you are supposed to eat together.

Peachtree: 5158 Ararat Drive, Kansas City, MO 64129
816-924-2929
www.peachtreerestaurants.com

Niecie's: 6441 Troost Avenue, Kansas City, MO 64131
816-444-6006
www.nieciesrestaurant.com

ROCK
ON THE PORCH

KC is a chance to walk some of the city's historic
ods and listen to local musicians. This is Kansas
ion of a block party and features food trucks and
ts. Check out on foot or bike. In 2014, the West Plaza
od hosted the event.

Porchfest KC:
www.porchfestkc.com
Neighborhood: West Plaza

MUSIC AND ENTERTAINMENT

Porchfest
neighborho
City's vers
visual artis
neighborh

CATCH A SHOW
AND A MEAL

Dinner and a movie? How about at the same time? Just across the state line, Standees theater and restaurant offers both, and those looking for a date night or just an innovative experience should check it out. Take food and drinks into the theater with you or have a meal before the show. Find a classy environment, clean restrooms and an alcoholic beverage during the big feature. It's the adult way to watch one of the latest movies.

Standees: 3935 West 69th Terrace, Prairie Village, KS 66208
913-601-5250
www.standeeseatery.com/prairie-village/movies

SEE
A MOONLIGHT PRODUCTION

Feel the warm breeze of a summer night and get a seat to watch one of the musical performances that come to this amphitheater in Swope Park. Popular productions like Seven Brides for Seven Brothers and the Sound of Music have weeklong showings, and other popular country and contemporary artists regularly have concerts at Kansas City Starlight Theatre. Talented actors and singers who have left Kansas City often find welcome homecomings when they return with one of the acts.

Kansas City Starlight Theater: 4600 Starlight Road, Kansas City, MO 64132
816-363-7827
www.kcstarlight.com

HAIL,
AND WELL MET!

Where can you walk around gnawing on a turkey leg while wearing a flower tiara? That would be the annual Kansas City Renaissance Festival in Bonner Springs. From the moment you step inside you'll meet people in character—wenches bursting at the bosom and ladies whose greetings will have you consulting your Olde English app. It's all part of the charm as you sway to the melody of a dulcimer like the motion of leaves up above while realizing that sadly, yes, in a former life, you probably would have been a peasant.

Kansas City Renaissance Fair:
www.kcrenfest.com

LISTEN
TO ALL THAT JAZZ

So you know about Kansas City jazz, but do you really? It's time to get those tickets for intimate performance at the Blue Room in the historic 18th and Vine District. It's easy to think about a time when men and women wearing formal attire snuck into the smoky rooms in clubs around here during Prohibition while politicians looked the other way. For larger concerts with a stage performance try the Gem Theater, which brings acts from all over. Head downtown to former speakeasy, the Phoenix, or midtown's popular Green Lady Lounge, to catch other local jazz-influenced acts.

Gem Theater: 1615 East 18th Street, Kansas City, MO 64108
816-474-8463

Blue Room: 1616 East 18th Street, Kansas City, MO 64108
816-474-2929
www.americanjazzmuseum.org

The Phoenix Jazz Club: 302 West 8th Street, Kansas City, MO 64105
816-221-5299
www.thephoenixkc.com

Green Lady Lounge: 1809 Grand Boulevard, Kansas City, MO 64108
816-215-2954
www.greenladylounge.com

INSIDER TIP

Minors are allowed at Blue Room performances as long as they are accompanied by an adult.

INTERESTING FACT

Kansas City Royals' Eric Hosmer invited friends to party with him at the Power & Light District after the baseball team advanced to the American League championship in 2014. He and other teammates bought everyone at McFadden's a drink to celebrate the victory.

BE PART
OF THE CROWD

A rebirth in Kansas City's downtown area is partly owed to the creation of what is called the Power & Light District, which beckons revelers to bars and restaurants in an eight-block stretch along Main Street. On weekends the crowd tends to run to twenty- and thirty-somethings, who stay late for the clubs, but the convenience of all the pubs and eateries together works for about anyone when looking for nightlife in the heart of the city. Festivities often spill out from one establishment to the next, creating a seamless pub crawl. One thing to look for is the town's biggest parties whenever there is a huge sporting event. Stage Live in the Power & Light District hosts watch opportunities for Royals' postseason play and drew thousands midday during the US 2014 World Cup games.

Power & Light District:
www.powerandlightdistrict.com
Neighborhood: Downtown

GET
YOUR CRAIC ON

Practice your Irish brogue and slang, and you'll fit right into Kansas City's strong Emerald Isle contingency. Perhaps it stems from the immigrant workers who made their homes in the West Bottoms and took many industrial and laboring jobs as the city grew in the early nineteen hundreds.

Explore Union Station's Irish Center, which can help track those ancestors back to the old country and teach you how to say "thank you" ("go raibh maith agat") in Irish. Then there's the annual Irish Fest at Crown Center. Earlier in the day the crowds are less and the music leans toward the traditional, yet you can get close enough to the stage to talk to artists and musicians who make their way from overseas, as well as homegrown Irish acts.

Irish Center: Union Station
www.unionstation.org/venues/irish-center

Irish Fest: Crown Center
www.kcirishfest.com

INSIDER TIP

*Find a seat early for Friday and
Saturday night headliners
at Irish Fest.*

FOR
ART'S SAKE

Kansas City's art scene is alive and vibrant, as is seen in the thriving neighborhoods of the Crossroads and West Bottoms. Artists find space in smaller galleries bolstered by bigger art names such as Lyric Opera of Kansas City, Kansas City Ballet, and the profound architectural wonder that is the Kauffman Center for the Performing Arts. In the nearby West Bottoms, the art takes a different form in vintage and antique finds at popular Good JuJu, where you'll discover restored furniture with a hip vibe. One of the best times to check out what's going on is during First Friday evenings, when the public is invited to stroll from gallery to boutique to see the latest installations while soaking up street entertainment in the Crossroads. The next morning, West Bottoms becomes the destination, with the warehouses open for shoppers looking for repurposed and retro goods.

Lulu's Thai Noodle Shop: 2030 Central Street, Kansas City, MO 64108
816-474-8424

Crossroads:
www.kccrossroads.org

West Bottoms:
www.westbottoms.com

INSIDER TIP

Town Topic and Lulu's Thai Noodle Shop in the Crossroads are perfect places for a quick bite as you explore the Crossroads District, especially during First Friday walks.

TRY
AN ALFRESCO VIEWING

Sit back and watch a movie from the comfort of your car. Or better yet, snuggle beneath a blanket in your camp chair in front of your car. An old-fashioned drive-in movie experience is guaranteed at Boulevard Drive-In. Double- and triple-feature billings are common—so be prepared. They have refreshments for purchase, but they'll let you bring your cooler if you like.

Boulevard Drive-In: 1051 Merriam Lane, Kansas City, KS 66103
913-262-0392
wwwboulevarddrivein.com/wordpress/

INSIDER TIP

Keep an eye out for events at Boulevard Drive-In because their listings aren't made far in advance.

HOLD
YOUR BREATH!

It's like yoga, the circus, and Cirque du Soleil acrobatics all in one, but the performances are unlike any others. The Kansas City troupe melds original music and fashion into an art form interspersing beauty and harmony. Go see for yourself this troupe that is making its name across the country through its "artistic athleticism." Local performances are becoming more rare as the troupe's popularity takes it to other cities. Keep an eye out for the next show.

Quixotic School of Performing Arts: 1616 Broadway Boulevard,
Kansas City, MO 64108
www.quixoticfusion.com

TIP
Try the aerial silk and trapeze for yourself
as you get others together for a party at
the Quixotic School of Performing Arts.

SPORTS AND RECREATION

SEE THE CITY
BY BIKE

Feel the wind in your hair and get your heart rate going as you explore the city, by bike.

B-Cycle is a bicycle sharing program in which you swipe your credit card at any of the dozens of stations across the metro area and—presto! You have a scenic and convenient ride to your next destination. The program is a partnership between BikeWalkKC and Blue Cross and Blue Shield of Kansas City to promote clean and healthy transportation. Tourists might find this method cheap and handy, but it also is growing among the local crowd, who use it for short trips and errands.

Kansas City B-Cycle: 208 West 19th Street, Kansas City, MO
816-205-7056
www.kansascity.bcycle.com

WHEN
IN KC

Only Rome has more fountains than we do, or so the bragging rights go. It's a good argument because if you start looking, you'll find them everywhere. Perhaps the most famous is the J.C. Nichols Memorial Fountain near the Country Club Plaza, an iconic spot to take a selfie, wedding, or family photograph. Some of our favorites include the Children's Fountain at Oak Trafficway and Burlington or the simplistic marble Armour Gardens one at 69th Street at Grand and Rockhill, which J.C. Nichols bought in Italy.

Kansas City Fountains:
www.kcfountains.com

GET LOST
IN SWOPE PARK

You can find at least a dozen reasons to visit Swope Park. This 1,800-acre green space is home to other spots that make the list, but it's worth a drive to see other, lesser known attractions like the new Soccer Village, disc golf course, and popular Kansas City Zoo, Starlight Theatre, and Lakeside Nature Center. Pack a picnic and find a quiet spot in the urban oasis.

Swope Park: Kansas City, MO 64132
816-513-7500
www.kcparks.org/park/swope-park/

FEED THE FISH
AND DUCKS AT LONGVIEW

Feed the dozens and dozens of carp that beg for food pellets at scenic Longview Lake, next to the Lee's Summit area marina. While there, look for blue herons, mallard, and white ducks, which are happy to take whatever leftover fish food you toss them. Rent a pontoon for a lakeside spin or find a quiet spot for fishing at this well-managed suburban park.

Longview Lake Park: 11100 View High Drive, Kansas City, MO 64134
www.jacksongov.org/

HIKE
IN QUIET

It's worth the drive to Parkville for a quiet hike that includes the Old Kate Trail and Parkville Nature Sanctuary. It's a short, easy walk that goes through a diverse landscape where deer and wild turkey often can be seen. It's perfect for a stroll to clear the head and relieve a bit of stress. Little legs can make the journey, too.

Parkville Nature Sanctuary: 9th and 12th Streets, Parkville, MO 64152
816-741-7676
www.parkvillenaturesanctuary.net

FEED
THE GOATS

No matter where you live in the metro area, Deanna Rose Children's Farmstead is a quick escape to the farm. This destination, named for the first Overland Park police officer killed in the line of duty, is popular with the younger crowd because of its pedal tractors and easy petting access to cows and goats. Regular milking demonstrations and hand-held bottle feeding for goats allow urban kids to see how a farm works. Make sure you get a bottle for the little kids "maaaa"ing at your knees.

Deanna Rose Children's Farmstead: 13800 Switzer Road,
Overland Park, KS 66221
913-897-2360
www.opkansas.org

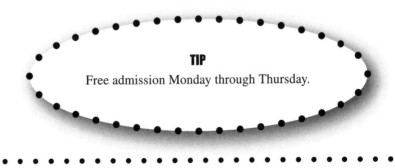

TIP
Free admission Monday through Thursday.

HAVE
A WILD TIME

Lakeside Nature Center is set back enough from busy Gregory Boulevard that some people drive on thinking the intentional prairie grass setting circles an abandoned building. Don't make that mistake. Stop and park. Inside, you'll find a collection of regional amphibians, reptiles, and birds enclosed and easy to view. The Center keeps eagles and falcons in a large outside cage. Make sure to hike the surrounding trails, which include forest, marsh, and limestone bluffs—all amazingly close to the city.

Lakeside Nature Center: 4701 East Gregory Boulevard,
Kansas City, MO 64132
816-513-8960
www.lakesidenaturecenter.org

GET
AWAY

Step softly as the mighty Missouri roars beneath during a hike at Weston Bend State Park, the most scenic trail in the area. Fall and winter are the best times to go as the foliage color pops and the gaps left by leaves frame the bubbling river water. Once you're in the area, head downtown to see Weston's quaint shops and antiques, wineries, or brewing company. You'll find enough of interest to spend all day walking the town's neighborhoods or exploring the countryside by car.

Weston Bend State Park: 16600 Missouri 45, Weston, MO 64098
816-640-5443
www.mostateparks.com
www.westonmo.com

STROLL
AN URBAN GARDEN

Take a break from shopping at the Country Club Plaza to explore the grounds of the Anita B. Gorman Discovery Center, maintained by the Missouri Department of Conservation. Frogs and turtles pop their heads above the pond set amid the nearby roads packed with restaurants and college campus buildings. This area, known as the Kaufmann Legacy Park, stretches across thirty-seven acres and is named for one of the most well-known philanthropic families.

Anita B. Gorman Discovery Center: 4750 Troost Avenue,
Kansas City, MO 64110
816-759-7300
www.mdc.mo.gov/regions/kansas-city/discovery-center

SINK
ONE IN

Putt-putt your heart out at the nostalgic Cool Crest Family Fun Center, a miniature golf course and entertainment area in Independence. This place ranks high in fond memories for many who grew up in the area. Ignore the tiny putter, because on that seventeenth green, with or without little ones in tow, you might as well be Rory McIlroy.

Cool Crest Family Fun Center: 10735 US Highway 40,
Independence, MO 64055
816-358-0088
www.coolcrest.com/home/

TAKE TIME
FOR THE RODEO

Nothing seems more of a quintessential Kansas City experience than the American Royal. This well-known event began in a tent in the old Kansas City Stockyards more than one hundred years ago. The horse show and rodeo grew over the years, garnering a reputation as one of the premier livestock competitions. It's a family-friendly event that now also includes a world-class barbecue competition.

American Royal: 1701 American Royal Court, Kansas City, MO 64102
816-221-9800
www.americanroyal.com

SLED DOWN
LIKE YOU KNOW WHAT'S UP

Before the first inch of snow has collected kids and "older kids" are locating their sledding spheres and tricked-out rides and heading to "Suicide Hill" in Brookside, south of the Plaza. It's a rite of passage for youngsters who have grown up anywhere near this park hill between 53rd and 54th Streets and Brookside Boulevard. The tradition continues, and whether it's an inch or foot, you'll find good company on the inclines.

INDULGE
IN SOME ROYAL TREATMENT

Kansas City baseball fans endured a major drought from the mid-1980s until 2014, when their home team Royals clawed their way into the World Series, the first time in nearly thirty years. Before that, tickets at the K (Kaufmann Stadium) were cheap and easy to get. It might be a bit more difficult now, but there is still a reason to go see them play. You'll be sitting among the nicest baseball fans in one of the most attractive ballparks—with a spacious outfield cascading fountain.

Kaufmann Stadium: One Royal Way, Kansas City, MO 64129
816-921-8000
www.royals.com

BE
A FÚTBOL FAN

Cheer for soccer even during non–World Cup years at Kansas City's Sporting Park, home of Major League Soccer champions Sporting Kansas City. We Kansas Citians proudly call our city "Soccer Capital of America," and Sporting jerseys and sportswear rival Royals and Chiefs logos on city and suburban streets. Go to the park and chant along with "We believe that we will win!" These guys can play!

Sporting Park: One Sporting Way, Kansas City, KS 66111
913-912-7600
www.sportingkc.com

PICK
YOUR OWN

A sunburn, sweat-soaked shirts, and calloused fingers are a small price to pay for fresh berries that can be plopped into oatmeal and cereal or cooked into jam. Kansas City offers many options for pick-your-own blueberries, strawberries, and blackberries. We like the Berry Patch's rows of blueberry bushes and adjacent country store, where you can buy already-picked berries to stick in your freezer. The best time to pick is a weekday morning. Not only will you miss the weekend crowds, you could avoid the heat.

Berry Patch: 22509 State Line Road, Cleveland, MO 64734
816-618-3771
www.pickyourown.org/MOkc.htm

TAKE YOURSELF OUT
TO THE BALLGAME

Go front and center and hear the crack of the bat yourself at a Kansas City T-Bones game. An evening with the indie professional league is a fun and affordable way to spend the evening whether you are a baseball fan or you have little ones who will appreciate the antics of the team's mascot or take a break at the playground and bounce house near the field.

American Community Ballpark: 1800 Village West Parkway,
Kansas City, KS 66111
www.tbonesbaseball.com

OBSERVE JAYHAWKS
IN THEIR NATURAL HABITAT

"Beware the Phog" is the saying of University of Kansas hoops fans. They are referring to Allen Fieldhouse, named for the Jayhawks' infamous coach Phog Allen. Indiana might have Hollywood basketball cred, but KU has the pedigree. Basketball inventor James Naismith established the university's program and was its first coach. The Phog is a basketball court with one of the best home advantages because of the noise level of the crowd and the institutional roundball insanity that flows through local drinking water.

Allen Fieldhouse: 1651 Naismith Dive, Lawrence, KS 66044
785-864-3141
www.kuathletics.com

FIND OUT
ABOUT ALL THE HOOPLA

Even if you already know who Jimmy V. was or who Michael Jordan played for in his co-ed days, you'll appreciate the College Basketball Experience at the Sprint Center—devoted to college basketball. It's connected to the Sprint Center and is an extension of Kansas City's basketball-loving atmosphere that has been home to scores of NCAA tournament and conference championship games over the years. Wear your Chuck T All-Stars or dig out those Nike Airs, because this place is part interactive, and visitors can shoot around or participate in a pick-up game or free-throw contest.

College Basketball Experience: Sprint Center, 1401 Grand Boulevard, Kansas City, MO 64106
816-949-7100
www.collegebasketballexperience.com

BLEED
RED

No, the National Anthem doesn't end with ". . . . and the home of the Chiefs," but thousands of fans will have you believing that. It's been a while since the Chiefs won a Super Bowl—1970 to be exact—yet the diehards come to the home games and arrive early. Make sure to find a tailgate spot amid the pop-up parties. No one knows how to grill in a parking lot quite like the people who list barbecue among their essential food groups.

Arrowhead Stadium: One Arrowhead Drive, Kansas City, MO 64129
816-920-9300
www.kcchiefs.com

MAKE A SPLASH
AND DEFY GRAVITY

Scream your way down the world's largest waterside, Verrückt (meaning "insane" in German) at Schlitterbahn Kansas City Waterpark. This slide is actually taller than the Statue of Liberty and Niagara Falls, with speeds reaching sixty-five mph. Testing rafts went flying, but the engineering has been fine-tuned so much that technicians orchestrate everything from the collective weight of raft participants to Velcro seat belts to keep riders safe. Brace yourself for the ride!

Schlitterbahn Kansas City Waterpark: 9400 State Avenue,
Kansas City, KS 66112
913-312-3110
www.schlitterbahn.com/kansas-city

NATURAL BEAUTY

CROSS
THE PRAIRIE

Powell Gardens has it all—from beautiful plants and flowers arising from a natural backdrop to sculptures and art exhibits. This botanical garden is approximately forty miles east of Kansas City. The popular Festival of Butterflies is held in late summer, when the conservatory is in a flurry of colorful flapping wings.

Powell Gardens: 1609 Northwest US Highway 50, Kingsville, MO 64061
816-697-2600
www.powellgardens.org

INSIDER TIP

Make the trek through the woodlands and wildflowers to the Marjorie Powell Allen Chapel amid its tranquil setting.

FIND
AN URBAN OASIS

Contemplate your next Kansas City adventure at Loose Park. This is the city's equivalent of Central Park, but instead of pricey highrises lining it, the large homes of the south Plaza region give it more of a residential feel. A running and walking loop circles the seventy-five acres. Go for a stroll or find a quiet corner in the Laura Conyers Smith Municipal Rose Garden. History and Civil War buffs can ponder the park as the site of the Battle of Westport.

Loose Park: 5200 Pennsylvania Avenue, Kansas City, MO 64112
816-784-5300
www.kcparks.org/park/loose-park/

HEAD
FOR THE FARM

Pull up to Weston Red Barn and every dream about moving to the country appears before your eyes. Red Barn—check. Rolling hills—check. Apple orchard—check. Cider donuts and hot chocolate for a hay ride that takes you to a pumpkin patch to you pick your own—check, check, and check. Chickens and other livestock on hand for viewing just add to the ambience. Show up right when it opens in the fall, and you can have the place all to yourself plus the chance to witness morning dew dotting the crimson and gold.

Weston Red Barn: 16300 Wilkerson Road, Weston, MO 64098
816-386-5437
www.westonredbarnfarm.com

CHEER ON
THE KANGAROOS

Kansas City's state college location UMKC (University of Missouri-Kansas City) is located in the heart of the town, southeast of the Country Club Plaza. Soccer and basketball games are affordable and get you right on the field or court to watch Division I college purity that comes with a love of the game minus TV timeouts or the pressures of pro scouting.

University of Missouri–Kansas City Athletics: 5100 Rockhill Drive, Kansas City, MO 64110
www.umkckangaroos.com

INSIDER TIP

These are affordable, fun family outings, and it's easy to acquire tickets and find parking.

FLY ABOVE
AN AFRICAN SAVANNAH

That African safari is likely years away, and your savings are going to retirement or future college funds. Don't worry— you can still see the savannah and watch the animals in the wild, through a simulated trip. Kansas City Zoo is a popular destination for many visitors and locals for the reasons zoos are big hits everywhere. If the zoo was high school, the polar bears Nikita and Berlin and the penguins would be its homecoming court. Ride the Sky Safari, a ski lift-like ride above the simulated Africa grasslands to watch giraffes, zebras, and ostriches below as you glide through the air. Check out special deals with "ride" options if you plan to catch the train, tram, or Sky Safari. You'll save money in one package rather than paying as you go.

Kansas City Zoo: 6800 Zoo Drive, Kansas City, MO 64132
816-595-1234
www.kansascityzoo.org

CULTURE AND HISTORY

STUDY
THE PUBLIC MURALS

The murals tell a story all their own, and it won't take long to spot a few paintings on warehouse brick or parking garage concrete. A drive near the downtown area reveals a Kansas City Monarchs team lineup at the Paseo YMCA in the eighteenth and Vine District. The city's first days are drawn at Union Station's Main Post Office, and River Market has a tribute to explorers Lewis and Clark. A painted wall at Main and Truman Road celebrates the city's connection to jazz. Other artists have projects around the metro area, too, like the 42nd Street mural project, featuring graffiti and street art.

LET
YOUR HAIR DOWN

The ubiquity of hair can still mean it has a special place in a museum, especially if it's as quirky as Leila's Hair Museum in Independence. Wreaths made of hair entertained with jewelry are framed and hung with stories that claim they are made from the locks of Marilyn Monroe, Queen Victoria, and Michael Jackson. Owner Leila Cohoon has purchased pieces for the collection over the years and is on a quest for more to include in the bracelets, broaches, and other adornments made with and inspired by human hair.

Leila's Hair Museum: 1333 South Noland Road, Independence, MO 64055
816-833-2955
www.leilashairmuseum.net

HOP A RIDE
ON A STREET CAR

Taxis are so nineteen hundreds. Kansas City's most modern venture into public transportation comes in the form of street cars, and this mode has a rich history in Kansas City. An underground metal cable replaced the mule- and horse-drawn cars in the late eighteen hundreds. That incarnation of streetcars ended in the late 1950s. However, sixty years later urbanites pushed for the KC Downtown Streetcar project and a route that would connect north and south along Main Street. It streamlines the urban core's biggest destinations from the Crown Center and Union Station to the Crossroads Art District and downtown's Power & Light District to the River Market. More tracks and destinations are sure to come.

KC Downtown Streetcar:
816-804-8882
www.kcstreetcar.org

GET
TO THE TOP

One of the lesser-known lookout spots is the scenic view from the thirtieth floor of the city hall. Visitors can walk the entire perimeter of the roof and look out from one of downtown's tallest buildings. Keep in mind parking downtown and take your time.

City Hall: 414 East 12th Street, Kansas City, MO 64106
www.kcmo.org
Neighborhood: Downtown

DRIVE
THROUGH WHIMSICAL NUTTERVILLE

Victorian houses found in the hidden enclave dubbed "Nutterville" set new rules for exterior paint—bright pink, pastel yellow with red trim, blood orange, and green. This collection of eccentric homes in midtown near Westport and north of the Plaza are offices for a wide array of small businesses, all under the lease management of James B. Nutter & Company. Nutter Sr. started the color scheme following an inspirational trip to artist neighborhoods in Telluride, Colorado. A beloved landlord, Nutter and his company are notorious for their efforts over the years to help people find homes in the urban core.

Directions: Take West 41st Street east of Broadway and turn onto Central or Baltimore. You'll be in the heart of Nutterville.

REMEMBER

Kansas Citians took the initiative to build the Liberty Memorial when World War I ended, and the 32,000-square-foot museum followed. Be prepared to spend time here and feel moved by the placement of its symbolic designs, such as the glass walkway overlooking a field of red poppies representing the lives lost. Go to the top of the Liberty Memorial tower for an incredible view of the surrounding area.

Liberty Memorial: 100 West 26th Street, Kansas City, MO 64108
816-888-8100
www.theworldwar.org

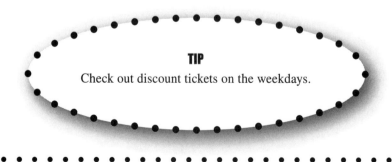

TIP
Check out discount tickets on the weekdays.

PAY YOUR RESPECTS
TO CHARLIE "BIRD" PARKER

He moved to Kansas City when he was a child, but Charlie Parker's name comes up immediately when someone refers to Kansas City jazz. He developed his art form here among the clubs that were home to the tunes of the day. Parker left to play gigs in New York City and abroad, but the notorious saxophonist and developer of the "bop" style known in jazz came home to rest. He is buried in Lincoln Cemetery at 8604 East Truman Road.

Lincoln Cemetery: 8500 Missouri 12, Kansas City, MO 64126

STUDY
AMERICAN INDIAN INFLUENCE

The people who were here first are remembered in the many names you'll find on the Kansas side of the metropolitan area—Shawnee, Shawnee Mission—used for towns, streets, and schools. One of the more comprehensive ways to see how settlers and natives interacted is at the Shawnee Indian Mission State Historic Site in Fairway. Study the baskets and drums and contemplate the times when tribes of American Indians called the area home.

Shawnee Indian Mission State Historic Site: 3403 West 53rd Street,
Fairway, KS 66205
913-262-0867
www.kshs.org/shawnee_indian

LEARN MORE
ABOUT THE AFRICAN-AMERICAN PIONEERS AT BRUCE WATKINS

The black community is one of the cornerstones of Kansas City, and the Bruce R. Watkins Cultural Heritage Center, which is named for the first African-American city councilman, brings this history to the forefront. It is situated where Swope Parkway turns to Blue Parkway and opened more than twenty-five years ago. The entire grounds are a tribute to the black legacy, including a foundation, Satchel Paige Stadium, and a picturesque hillside. Browse works from local and regional artists who house exhibits there, like the recent "Freedom Fighter" exhibit about Buffalo Soldiers during the Civil War.

Bruce R. Watkins Cultural Heritage Center: 3700 Blue Parkway,
Kansas City, MO 64130
816-784-4444
www.kcmo.org/parks

WALK
WHERE THE OUTLAWS DID

They fired shots into the cold February afternoon and fled with their loot, leaving one dead. So goes the story of the infamous James gang at a bank in Liberty's historic square in 1866. Jesse James and his posse had ties to the area because the family home is nearby, so the escape with the estimated $60,000 was an easy one. Travel north to see the Jesse James Bank Museum or tour the family's home at the farm that "Friends of the James Family" restored when they purchased it from the outlaws' descendants.

Jesse James Bank Museum: 103 North Water, Liberty, MO 64068
816-736-8510
www.claycountymo.gov/Historic_Sites/Jesse_James_Bank_Museum

Friends of the James Farm: 21216 James Farm Road, Kearney, MO 64068
816-736-8500
www.jessejames.org

PEEK
AT THE SHADY PAST

Look beyond the friendly faces of Kansas City today and there's a seedy history that few of these nice Midwesterners like to admit. Back in the 1920s and 1930s, gangsters called the shots around town and had so much clout that the feds had to step in and clean things up. Even native US President Harry S. Truman owed the beginnings of his political career to boss Tom Pendergast. Although it doesn't guarantee to show you where the bodies are buried, this tour will get you thinking about the days when gangsters called some of the political shots in Kansas City. Join your group at Union Station for a drive to the area establishments and spots that housed the mobsters who once ran the Kansas City scene.

Groups and Tours in Kansas City: 1300 Lydia, Kansas City, MO 64106
816-471-1234
www.thekctours.com/gangster-tour.html
Neighborhood: Midtown

EXPLORE
IN THE FOOTSTEPS OF
LEWIS AND CLARK

Channel Lewis and Clark in the suburb of Independence. The famous pair passed through the area and sent word of fantastic sites and likely had more OMG! experiences than we could ever imagine. They camped in the region before setting off on their Missouri River adventure.

Independence claims the starting point for other pioneers and is known for the beginning of the California, Oregon, and Santa Fe trails that took settlers westward. We suggest starting at National Frontier Trails Museum to do a bit of your own exploring.

National Frontier Trails Museum: 318 West Pacific Avenue,
Independence, MO 64050
816-325-7575
www.ci.independence.mo.us/nftm/

WATCH
THE FLAMES

You won't get burned when you join the others amid the free artistic fest that involves Barnaby Evan's Waterfire art installation as the flames light up Brush Creek south of the Plaza. The annual fall weekend brings musical and other performing artists to provide entertainment to those along the water's edge. Shows feature theater acts and dance, along with an eclectic mix of cultural music that coincides with the more than fifty floating fiery works. The art shows are part of Evans' experiment using public space.

Waterfire: Country Club Plaza, 4750 Broadway, Kansas City, MO 64112
816-753-0100
www.waterfirekc.com

INSIDER TIP

Many of Kansas City's grocery stores have coupons that will help save on admission price.

SEE
PIGS RACE

More than a pumpkin patch awaits at Carolyn's Country Cousins. Hop on for a train ride and see the petting zoo or sink your teeth into the kettle korn, fudge, or pumpkin donuts—a must try! Then stick around and watch the swine sprint around their pen in Uncle Lester's races.

Carolyn's Country Cousins: 17607 Northeast 52nd Street,
Liberty, MO 64068
816-781-9196
www.carolynscountrycousins.com

WALK BACK
IN TIME

Eighty acres welcomes visitors to an old homestead that is Shoal Creek Living History Museum. Although the buildings were relocated to this setting from surrounding counties, they fit just right into a village straight from the eighteen hundreds. Walk the grounds free of charge on a random day with a self-guided tour, or seek out one of the special events—harvest festival, Civil War, and other re-enactments. Keep your eyes peeled for the wandering buffalo.

Shoal Creek Living History Museum: 7000 Northeast Barry Road,
Kansas City, MO 64156
816-792-2655
www.shoalcreeklivinghistorymuseum.com

PEEK INSIDE
AN ARTIST'S STUDIO

Thomas Hart Benton had already made a name for himself as a famous muralist by the time he returned to teach at the Kansas City Art Institute. He found inspiration in the agrarian life that was the Midwest and depicted the struggles that farmers had with the ongoing industrialization. His most famous mural is in Missouri's capitol and highlights the scars of slavery and organized crime amid the bucolic landscape. Missouri State Parks department has preserved the artist's home and studio in midtown and allows visitors to tour.

Missouri State Parks:
800-334-6946
www.mostateparks.com/park/thomas-hart-benton-home-and-studio-state-historic-site

BRUSH UP
ON DESIGN

Church members of the Community Christian Church near the Plaza had a request when their former building burned down in the late 1930s. They wanted architectural icon Frank Lloyd Wright to design a new building. He did so and used his parallelogram design, and the church added the intended "spire of light" at a later date. Tours are free and open to the public. Other Frank Lloyd Wright buildings include the Frank Bott Residence at 3640 Northwest Briarcliff Road and the Clarence Sondern House at 3600 Belleview Avenue.

GO MOD
FOR ART

Close to the Kansas City Art Institute classrooms is the Kemper Museum of Contemporary Art. The main building is home to traveling exhibits that can range from wall-sized photographs to video installations or the works of a Chinese painter. Don't forget to check out the building holding the permanent Bebe and Crosby Kemper Collection, including works from Georgia O'Keefe and Dale Chihuly. Another gallery, Kemper at the Crossroads, is smaller and also open to the public.

Kemper Museum of Contemporary Art: 4420 Warwick Boulevard,
Kansas City, MO 64111
816-753-5784
www.kemperart.org

TIP
A gallery is transformed to a story time venue with Tots on Tuesdays held on the third Tuesday of the month.

BUMP YOUR NOSE
ON THE GLASS

Mind your step and wander the maze that is the glass labyrinth at the Nelson-Atkins Museum of Art, a more recent addition commissioned by the Hall Family Foundation. It's an interactive display and invites the public to participate in navigating the way through the large-scale triangulated puzzle. One of the best parts is laughing at the little ones trying to find their way. Then go inside and tour the Nelson itself or tour the grounds with the giant shuttlecocks and other works in the sculpture park that surrounds the museum. Access to everything is free daily.

Nelson-Atkins Museum of Art: 4525 Oak Street, Kansas City, MO 64111
816-751-1278
www.nelson-atkins.org

FIND
INNER PEACE

Serenity's zip code is 64065 in the tiny community of Unity Village, southeast of Kansas City. Nearly one hundred people live here full time, but dozens more come annually for retreats open to all faiths and lifestyles. The village was created nearly one hundred years ago as a getaway for those of the Unity spiritual movement, and its open, accepting atmosphere and immaculate grounds can be a calming site. Comb through the campus library and archives, which contain metaphysical journals and books you won't find elsewhere.

Unity Village: 1901 Northwest Blue Parkway, Unity Village, MO 64065
816-251-3554
www.unity.org

SHOW UP
FOR THE SHOW

Lyric Opera in the eastern edge of the Crossroads continues to garner an increasingly larger following as word spreads about its performances, made for metropolitan areas much larger than Kansas City. Watch a moving opera in its original language. Check out upcoming productions at the First Friday open houses that are part of the first weekend's art events.

Lyric Opera of Kansas City: 1725 Holmes Street, Kansas City, MO 64108
816-471-4933
www.kcopera.org

TOUR
A THROWBACK TOWN

Your inner Laura Ingalls Wilder needs to check out Missouri Town 1855. Its structures are part of Jackson County Parks and Recreation. During the warmer months you can check out what a farming community was like in the mid-eighteen hundreds. Professional historical interpreters and actors add to the ambience. You can walk through and see livestock, and younger visitors can learn about a self-sustaining farm or see a blacksmith in action. Keep a lookout for the fall festival.

Missouri Town 1855: 8010 East Park Road, Blue Springs, MO 64064
816-503-4860
www.jacksongov.org/missouritown/

LEARN
ABOUT THE MORMON SETTLEMENT

The Garden of Eden, according to the Church of Latter-Day Saints, was located near the suburb of Independence. Missionaries later settled in the area, and the region has held much significance for the church. The public can view details on the church's history and read about its discriminated past as followers were pushed westward, at a visitors center, which has long been rumored to be the spot for a future LDS temple.

Visitors' Center: 937 West Walnut Street, Independence, MO 64051
816-836-3466
www.lds.org/locations/independence-visitors-center

SCAT
LIKE YOU MEAN IT

Yes, we are here, smack in the middle of the heartland, but ask anyone in Kansas City—jazz is the city's sound. The town's connection to jazz is documented at the American Jazz Museum in the Historic 18th and Vine District. Walk through the hallways and read how Count Basie and Charlie Parker honed their talents at nearby clubs. This is an educational trip, and one of our favorite times to She-Be-Do-Bop-Bop to the museum is for Jazz Storytelling in the museum's atrium, when the little ones play rhythm games along with bass, drums, and jazz singers.

American Jazz Museum: 1616 East 18th Street, Kansas City, MO 64108
816-474-8463
www.americanjazzmuseum.org

SEE
CIVIL WAR-ERA ARCHITECTURE

Kansas City's Civil War history is bloody and as extensive as the Missouri-Kansas border, which became a literal dividing line for a symbolic split between Union sympathizers and slaveholding others. Two houses that survived the war included the John Wornall House, which was used as a hospital for Union and Confederate soldiers after the Battle of Westport, and the Alexander Majors House. Majors was a businessman who helped found the Pony Express. These homes have been preserved for public tours and events.

John Wornall House: 6115 Wornall Road, Kansas City, MO 64113
816-444-1858
www.wornallmajors.org/explore/majors-house/

Alexander Majors House and Barn: 8201 State Line Road,
Kansas City, MO 64114
816-444-1858
www.wornallmajors.org/explore/majors-house/

ROLL
WITH THE HOGS

So you won't get your motor running and head out on the highway, but you can go on a free factory tour at Harley-Davidson in Kansas City. These hour-long tours allow you to walk through the facility as technicians use lasers to cut parts for the bikes plus see the robotic systems used. A steel-toe tour for a price allows visitors a closer look at the factory's workings.

Harley-Davidson: 11401 North Congress Avenue, Kansas City, MO 64153
877-883-1450
www.harley-davidson.com/content/h-d/en_US/home/events/factory-tours/
kanascitymo.html

TAKE
A BIG LEAGUE TOUR

Players of the Negro League were performing acrobatic outfield plays and slamming homers long before Jackie Robinson, who also played for the Negro League's Kansas City Monarchs, broke Major League Baseball's color barrier. The collection of The Negro Leagues Baseball Museum stretches from the late eighteen hundreds to the 1960s and includes photographs and artifacts from the league's heyday. You can't leave without reading about Kansas City's beloved Buck O'Neil, who spent most of his time with the Monarchs and was a fixture in establishing the museum. Someone who works at the museum can likely tell you his or her own personal Buck O'Neil story.

Negro Leagues Baseball Museum: 1616 East 18th Street,
Kansas City, MO 64108
816-221-1920
www.nlbm.com

FIND
YOUR STORY

You know you are in Kansas City when you go to the library not just to pick up a book—although they have a lot of them—or attend a talk or event—and they bring some interesting ones—but you just want to go sit in a cool building. We are thinking of the Plaza Branch location and the Central library in downtown. The Plaza library offers a modern environment with huge windows that overlook the streets surrounding the shopping district. For the ultimate book worm, historian, or architecture fan, the Central location, with pillars in front, needs to be visited. Even if you don't pick up a book, walk in the entry way and see for yourself its ornate nooks, its archive collection and film vault.

Kansas City Libraries:
www.kclibrary.org

WATCH
IN A WORLD-CLASS WAY

Night or day, it's magical just to enter the Kaufmann Center for the Performing Arts. It took years to design and build this center because each detail was painstakingly made to create a world-class establishment. Take a public tour to walk through the lobby areas illuminated with light through huge glass panels. Or catch a performance at Helzburg Hall where the 5,000-pipe organ might just accompany a heavenly choir of angels in the acoustically perfect performance hall.

Kaufmann Center for the Performing Arts: 1601 Broadway Boulevard,
Kansas City, MO 64108
www.kauffmancenter.org

HAIL
TO THE CHIEF

Find out what the "S" means in President Harry S. Truman's name, among other trivia, when you visit the museum in Independence honoring Truman, Missouri's only president. It's a stop for many national traveling exhibits that can feature displays such as Cold War spies or the many broaches Secretary of State Madeline Albright wore depending on her mood. Of course there's also the permanent exhibit exploring Truman's life and presidential career.

Harry S. Truman Library and Museum: 500 US Highway 24,
Independence, MO 64050
816-268-8200
www.trumanlibrary.org

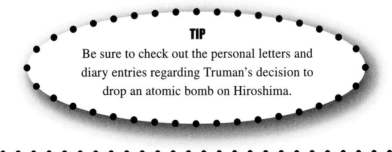

TIP
Be sure to check out the personal letters and diary entries regarding Truman's decision to drop an atomic bomb on Hiroshima.

UNCOVER
A TREASURE

It has the makings of a movie—a group of guys gets together and decides to dig for treasure in Missouri farmland. But that is the plot behind the story that is the Arabia Steamboat Museum. In fact, other steamboats are believed to be buried in ground that was once covered by the Missouri River. Take the tour in the historic River Market district that starts with the rising action of river travel history and westward expansion in the mid-eighteen hundreds, followed by the suspense of digging for the steamboat. Then enter a location that, in climatic fashion, showcases the settlers' near-perfectly preserved artifacts—Wedgwood china, shoes, boots, clothing, weapons, razors, doorknobs and more—brand-new household goods like out of an 1850s Macy's department store.

The Arabia Steamboat Museum: 400 Grand Boulevard,
Kansas City, MO 64106
816-471-1856
www.1856.com

IT'S
ELECTRIC

Throwback is the new present. So put on that apron, swing open the bamboo curtains, and cue Elvis Presley—you've entered the All-Electric House that is preserved from the 1950s. It's difficult to imagine that nineteen-inch TV screen was considered a big screen at the time. How times have changed. The exhibit is part of the Johnson County Museum.

Johnson County Museum: 6305 Lackman Road, Shawnee, KS 66217
913-715-2550
www.jocogov.org/dept/museum/home

LOOK UP
SOMETHING

In this information-devouring time it's nice to know you can kick it old-school, tell Google to get lost, and investigate original documents—yes! They exist! Kansas City is home to a National Archives location, and it regularly holds events on information and its usage ranging from Big Brother and Eric Snowden to Nazi propaganda effects. The most interesting items among the collection are court case records involving fugitive slave Dred Scott and Henry Ford of automobile fame.

National Archives: 400 West Pershing Road, Kansas City, MO 64108
816-268-8000
www.archives.gov/kansas-city/

ROLL
IN THE DOUGH

In our age of ATM cards and electronic payment, will our kids even think about paper and coin money? At the Money Museum of Kansas City's Federal Reserve Bank you can see a gold bar worth nearly a half-million dollars or design your own currency, which are both part of the tour. Of course, there's no value you can put on this experience—it's free.

The Money Museum at the Federal Reserve Bank of Kansas City:
One Memorial Drive, Kansas City, MO 64198
816-881-2683
www.kansascityfed.org/moneymuseum

SHOPPING AND FASHION

BE SEEN
AT THE SCENE

Summer Sunday afternoons attract the beautiful people to the Hotel Sorella rooftop pool for drinks, flirting, and maybe a bit of splash. Even if your abs aren't toned or biceps buff, the people-watching is top notch. The Jones rooftop pool in the Power & Light District offers similar eye candy, but membership has its privileges. So tie on a sarong, put on a ringer T, and slide on those sunglasses so no one knows where you are looking. You're not in Kansas City anymore.

Hotel Sorella Country Club Plaza: 901 West 48th Place,
Kansas City, MO 64112
816-753-8800
www.hotelsorella-countryclubplaza.com

GET
THE BLUES

What is it about those Baldwin blue jeans that has people in the fashion world yakking? It's the functionality and the way they look. Matt Baldwin honed his clothes manufacturing skills—yes, there is such a thing as apparel manufacturing skills in Los Angeles—but opened his boutique in Kansas City. Go to the original Leawood location or the shop on the Plaza. And get one of those KC Baldwin caps while you are at it. Homeboy entertainer Jason Sudeikis can't keep them all for himself.

Baldwin KC: 340 West 47th Street, Kansas City, MO 64112
913-312-2375
www.baldwindenim.com

WEAR YOUR HEART
ON YOUR SHIRT

Embrace your city-inspired fashion with a KC-heart T-shirt from local designer Charlie Hustle. This designer uses vintage-inspired ideas for soft T-shirts that feel good and reflect a modern vibe and even has some for your itty-bitty city cheerleaders. Or go for the crisscrossed KCMO Crossroads shirts found at Westport's Bunker store. Hometown pride is always in fashion here. We've noticed other T-shirt designers and screen printers are popping up all the time as the T-craze continues. Look for Sandlot Goods, Kansas City Bravery Company, Made Urban Apparel, and Normal Human, among others, for a shirt with character.

HEAD
FOR FASHION

Even your father, father-in-law, or cool uncle could use a dash of urban fashion. Choose from a wide selection of authentic flat caps that fold low and hug tight at Harold Pener "Man of Fashion." A Sunday-style suit and hat—that once in a lifetime purchase—is also found here. Mostly, it's a fun place to check out the latest in urban fashion, even if you don't buy anything. Try the iconic location on 63rd Street.

Harold Pener Man of Fashion: 1801 East 63rd Street,
Kansas City, MO 64131
816-363-1676

GO
UNDER

Birdies, in the Crossroads district, has intimate apparel that will delight but is tasteful and stylish. Just walking into the shop is a fashionable venture. They even have swimsuits in hard-to-find sizes. Plus, the employees know what's what and will help you break out of your rut and unleash the vixen within. Guys, you'll feel welcome trying to pick out a gift for the both of you or grabbing a gift certificate so she can surprise you.

Birdies: 116 West 18th Street, Kansas City, MO 64108
816-842-2473
birdiespanties.com

GRAB
CULTURE IN THE SUBURBS

Suburb Overland Park has marked a place on Kansas City's culture map with the opening of Prairiefire, a New York museum–inspired establishment with mixed uses. It houses permanent and traveling science-inspired art exhibits. But its upscale restaurants and sushi bar and entertainment facilities like Pinstripes Bowling give a person many reasons to visit. Go while the buzz is still building.

Prairiefire: 5661 West 135th Street, Overland Park, KS 66223
913-647-5160
www.visitprairiefire.com

HANG
WITH THE HIPSTERS

Westport earned reputations in decades past as the place to party or the place to get a tattoo, sometimes simultaneously. The coolness appeal still lingers with ever-in-fashion urban Bunker and Boomerang vintage apparel, but the area has redefined itself in other ways. A champagne bar and local microbrews are finding their way into restaurants, and the area is seeing an ever-changing eclectic mix. Try a burger at Green Room Burgers & Beer or go for small plates at simply elegant Bluestem. You won't have to go far for an after-dinner drink or dessert.

Green Room Burgers & Beer: 4010 Pennsylvania Avenue,
Kansas City, MO 64111
816-216-7682
www.greenroomkc.com

Bluestem: 900 Westport Road, Kansas City, MO 64111
816-561-1101
www.bluestemkc.com

READ
LIKE A CHILD

Stepping into Reading Reptile children's bookstore in Brookside is like stepping into your favorite book. Elaborate paper-mache characters from beloved books like *The Giving Tree* and *The Very Hungry Caterpillar* hang from the walls and ceiling. Children disappear into worn, comfortable chairs or a secret crawl space. It's a community center, birthday party venue, bakery, and art space—all in one. The owners will give you great advice about tried-and-trued books for younger ones to spark their imaginations. It's not always a book you've heard of—but you trust the owners' advice. Read A. Bitterman's blog on the store's website about children's literature and the modern book industry.

Reading Reptile: 328 West 63rd Street, Kansas City, MO 64113
816-753-0441
www.readingreptile.com

STRIDE
THROUGH THE PLAZA

Country Club Plaza, often shortened to Plaza by those in the know, was the brainchild of developer J.C. Nichols and inspired by the architecture of Seville, Spain. It is considered the first suburban shopping center. A nice spring, summer, or fall day makes this pedestrian-friendly area a likely destination to browse the many shops or grab a bite to eat. Around the holidays, the lights outlining the buildings make for a festive stroll. Giggle with the locals who find themselves singing the holiday song: "Cause it's Christmas, in Kansas City. Yes it's Christmas, everywhere. And the Plaza Lights are looking pretty. . . . Kansas City, I'll be there."

EAT LOCAL
AND FRESH

We are stuck between miles and miles of farmland, so a likely destination is a farmers' market, whether near a neighborhood or elsewhere. River Market on the weekend is grocery shopping and entertainment all in one. Taste fresh-baked bread from Bloom Baking Company while meandering among the local produce tables (keep to those in the center for true organic and regional items). Overland Park hosts another popular market that is a favorite for its variety and fierce loyalty to some of the vendors. Smaller neighborhood markets in Brookside and Waldo are nice stops as well.

City Market: 20 East 5th Street, Suite 201, Kansas City, MO 64106
816-842-1271
www.thecitymarket.org

Overland Park Farmers Market: 7950 Marty Street,
Overland Park, KS 66204
913-895-6000
www.opkansas.org/things-to-see-and-do/farmers-market/

Kansas City Food Circle:
www.kcfoodcircle.org/markets/

SHOP
FOR THROWBACK THREADS AND SPOTS TO POP A SQUAT

Vintage has a loyal following here, and a Saturday morning is the perfect time to check out the many venues around town. Our favorites are Urban Mining, a midtown staple that is usually open only the first weekend of the month, and Good JuJu in the West Bottoms. For that full-length fur or '60s boots, try Boomerang. Retro Inferno is for the deep-pockets vintage seeker who recognizes names and doesn't mind paying for them.

River Market Antiques: 115 West 5th Street, Kansas City, MO 64105
816-221-0220
www.rivermarketantiquemall.com

TLC Thrifty Boutique: 8025 Santa Fe Drive, Overland Park, KS 66204
913-461-3779

Good JuJu: 1420 West 13th Terrace, Kansas City, MO 64101
816-421-1930
www.goodjujukc.com

Boomerang: 3900 Pennsylvania Avenue, Kansas City, MO 64111
816-531-6111
www.boomerang-kc.com

Retro Inferno: 1500 Grand Boulevard, Kansas City, MO 64108
816-842-2004
www.retroinferno.com

SUGGESTED ITINERARIES

FAMILY FUN

American Royal, 59

Carolyn's Country Cousins, 95

Deanna Rose Farmstead, 54

Eat at Winstead's or Town Topic, 13

Feed the Ducks and Carp at Longview Lake, 52

Kansas City Zoo's Sky Safari, 76

Lakeside Nature Center, 50

Missouri Town 1855, 103

Reading Reptile, 124

Schlitterbahn Waterpark, 68

T-Bones Baseball Game, 64

The Money Museum at the Federal Reserve Bank, 115

FOR THE SPORTS FAN

Allen Fieldhouse, 65

Chiefs Game at Arrowhead Stadium, 67

College Basketball Experience Museum, 66

Negro Leagues Baseball Museum, 108

Royals Game at Kaufmann Stadium, 61

Sporting KC Game, 62

• •

MIX-IT-UP

Café Europa, 20

Drive through Nutterville, 85

Hang in Westport, 123

Leila's Hair Museum, 82

Nosh at a Gas Station, 3

Powell Gardens, 70

See the Excavated Arabia Steamboat, 112

A FOODIE FANTASY

Aixois Bistro, 20

Barbecue at Arthur Bryant's, LC's, and RJ's, 26

Christopher Elbow Chocolate, 8

Fluffy Fresh Donuts, 5

Garōzzo's, 12

Glacé, 8

KC Bier Company, 17

Local Pig, 16

Roasterie Coffee, 10

THIS IS KANSAS CITY?

Anton's Taproom, 4

Kansas City Renaissance Festival, 35

• •

Quixotic School of Performing Arts, 46
See the City by Bike, 48

HISTORY LESSON

All-Electric House, 113
American Jazz Museum, 105
Harry S. Truman Presidential Library, 111
Shawnee Indian Mission Museum, 88
Union Station and Mafia Tour, 91
World War I Museum, 86

NORTH OF THE RIVER ROAD TRIP

Belvoir Winery, 6
Harley-Davidson Tour, 107
Jesse James Bank Museum, 90
Shatto Milk Company Tour, 23
Weston Bend State Park, 56
Weston Red Barn, 73

GIRLS' NIGHT OUT

Bier Station, 17
Crossroads Art District First Fridays, 102

• •

Kaufmann Center for the Performing Arts, 110

Lyric Opera, 102

Snow & Co. Cocktails, 25

Standees Theater, 33

Starlight Theater, 34

KANSAS CITY FIX

American Royal, 59

Arthur Bryant's, 26

Country Club Plaza, 125

Gem Theater in 18th and Vine District, 36

Nelson-Atkins Museum of Art, 100

Tour the Fountains, 49

• •

ACTIVITIES
BY SEASON

WINTER

Cheer on the UMKC Kangaroos, 74

College Basketball Experience Museum, 66

Country Club Plaza Lights, 125

Kemper Museum of Contemporary Art, 99

Nelson-Atkins Museum of Art, 100

Union Station, 21

University of Kansas Allen Fieldhouse, 65

SPRING

Powell Gardens, 70

Tour the Fountains, 49

Longview Lake, 52

Parkville Nature Sanctuary, 53

Sporting KC Soccer Match, 62

Loose Park, 72

SUMMER

Berry Picking, 63

Boulevard Drive-In, 44

Boulevardia in the West Bottoms, 24

Farmers Markets, 126

• •

Hotel Sorella Pool, 117

Kansas City Zoo, 76

KC Irish Fest, 40

Royals Game, 61

Schlitterbahn Waterpark, 68

T-Bones Baseball Game, 64

FALL

Carolyn's Country Cousins, 95

Chiefs and Arrowhead Stadium, 67

Kansas City Renaissance Festival, 35

KC Bier Company—Octoberfest, 17

Missouri Town 1855 Fall Festival, 103

Shoal Creek Living History Museum, 96

Waterfire KC, 93

Weston Bend Day Trip (Weston Red Barn and Weston Bend State Park), 56, 73

INDEX

18th and Vine District, 36, 80, 105

75th Street Brewery, 14-15

Alexander Majors House, 106

All-Electric House, 113

Allen Fieldhouse, 65

American Jazz Museum, 105

Anton's Taproom, 4

Arabia Steamboat Museum, 112

Arrowhead Stadium, 67

Arthur Bryant's, 26-27

Baldwin, 118

Battle of Westport, 72, 106

B-Cycle, 48

Bean, John L. and Marsha, 6

Belvoir Winery, 6

Benton, Thomas Hart, 97

Berry Patch, 63

Bier Station, The, 17

BikeWalkKC, 48

Birdie's, 121

Bloom Baking Company, 126

Blue Room, 36

Boomerang, 123, 128

Boulevard Brewery, 15

Boulevard Drive-In, 44

Browne's Irish Market, 18

Bruce R. Watkins Cultural Heritage Center, 89

Brush Creek, 93

Bunker, 119, 123

Charlie Hustle, 119

Church of Latter-Day Saints, 104

Cinder Block Brewery, 14-15

City Hall, 84

City Market Coffee House, 10-11

Clarence Sodern House, 98

Coffee Girls, 10-11

College Basketball Experience, 66

Cool Crest, 58

Community Christian Church, 98

Christopher Elbow Artisanal Chocolates, 8

Crossroads Art District, 83

Crown Center, 21, 40, 83

Country Club Plaza, 49, 57, 74, 93, 117, 125

Deanna Rose Children's Farmstead, 54

Federal Reserve Bank of Kansas City, 115

Fiorella's Jack Stack Barbecue, 26

Fluffy Fresh Donuts, 5

Frank Bott Residence, 98

Garōzzo's, 12

Gates & Sons Bar-B-Q, 26-27

Gem Theater, 36

Good JuJu, 42, 128

Green Lady Lounge, 36

Green Room Burgers & Beer, 14-15, 123

Hall Family Foundation, 100

Harley-Davidson, 107

Harold Pener, 120

Harry S. Truman Library and Museum, 111

Hosmer, Eric, 38

Hotel Sorella, 117

Jack Stack, 26

James Farm, 90

Jesse James Bank Museum, 90

John's Space Age Donuts, 5

John Wornall House, 106

Kansas City Art Institute, 97, 99

Kansas City Ballet, 42

Kansas City Bravery Company, 119

Kansas City Chiefs, 67

Kansas City Public Library, 109

Kansas City Renaissance Festival, 35

Kansas City Royals, 39, 61

Kansas City Starlight Theatre, 34, 50

Kansas City T-Bones, 64

Kansas City Zoo, 50, 76

Kaufmann Center for the Performing Arts, 110

Kaufmann Legacy Park, 57

Kaufmann Stadium, 61

KC Bier Company, 17

KC Irish Fest, 40

Kemper Museum of Contemporary Art, 99

Lakeside Nature Center, 50, 55

LaMar's, 5

Laura Conyers Smith Municipal Rose Garden, 72

LC's Bar-B-Q, 27

Lewis and Clark, 80, 92

Liberty, 6, 8, 15, 68, 86, 90, 95

Leila's Hair Museum, 82

Lincoln Cemetery, 87

Local Pig, 16

Longview Lake, 52

Loose Park, 72

Lulu's Thai Noodle Shop, 42

Lyric Opera, 42, 102

Made Urban Apparel, 119

Margarita's Amigos, 19

Martin City Brewery, 14-15

McCoy's, 14-15

McFadden's, 38

Missouri River, 92, 112

Missouri Town 1855, 103

Money Museum, 115

Murray's Handmade Ice Creams, 9

National Archives, 114

National Frontier Trails Museum, 92

Negro Leagues Baseball Museum, 108

Nelson-Atkins Museum of Art, 100

• •

Niecie's, 28

Normal Human, 119

Nutterville, 85

Nutter, James B., 85

Oddly Correct, 10-11

Oklahoma Joe's, 3, 26

Old Kate Trail, 53

O'Neil, Buck, 108

Papu's, 3

Parker, Charlie "Bird", 87

Parkville Nature Sanctuary, 53

Paseo YMCA, 80

Parisi, 10-11

Peachtree Restaurants, 28

Phoenix Jazz Club, The, 36

Pierpont's, 21

Pizza 51 West, 3

Poco's, 19

Porchfest, 32

Powell Gardens, 70

Power and Light District, 39, 83, 117

Q39, 26

• •